Elisabethe Dupuy

The Queen's quire

Being a Book of Songs, Sonnets and Ballads

Elisabethe Dupuy

The Queen's quire
Being a Book of Songs, Sonnets and Ballads

ISBN/EAN: 9783744789264

Printed in Europe, USA, Canada, Australia, Japan

Cover: Foto ©Thomas Meinert / pixelio.de

More available books at **www.hansebooks.com**

The Queen's Quire:
Being a Book of Songs, Sonnets, and Ballads, written by Elisabethe Dupuy, Author of ∴ ∴ ∴ "The Dragon Yoke:" ∴ ∴ ∴ Dedicate to Cytherea. ∴ ∴ ∴

"and on the small grene twistes set

the lytel swete nightingales, and sung"

The Queen's Quire.

STAR OF LOVE.

Who calleth thee forth thro' azure shadows, dew-drip-
      ping, O Venus?
Star of Love, thy mellow glance entrances the heavens;
Thy beams shed tenderness, thou awakenest memories
      that slept,
    So that looking on thee I seem to feel again (sweet
      sorrow),
            Kisses ambrosial.

The pyre of the sun-widowed day glows with azure and
      amber;
Star of Love, thou leadest forward thy golden train;
Thy herald winds laugh in the tops of the silver-leaved
      poplars,
    So that listening to them I seem to hear the soft pipe,
      O Venus,
            Of Delphian Apollo.

The sound of sweet bells and murmuring waters is heard
      in the vale;
Star of Love, thou hast looked on the path where the
      red poppies blow;
Lo, the wings of thy white doves winnow the wine-
      spiced air,
    So that beholding their flight, I seem to be charioted,
      O Venus,
            Thro' the realm of Dreams.

Distil me the alembic of oblivion from the dew of red
    poppies;
Star of Love, by thy spell the tan-spotted leopard grows
    tame in his lair,
Likewise the proud heart of my lover melt with thine
    amorous fire,
So that thinking on me he shall seem as one drunken,
    O Venus,
              With the wine of delight.

AVILLON.

Oft when the moon hangs low against the blue,
    You see a golden pathway leading far
    O'er seas to Avillon, that like a star
Serene and distant, lures us to pursue
And yet eludes us, shining thro' the dew
    Of our salt tears, whose fitful gushings mar
    The symmetry of vision: such ways are
But roads that lead to isles which dreams imbrue.
On the horizon's utmost moony verge,
    Drenched with pale sea-foam, drifting, dusky, dim,
    Lies lilied Avillon, and in our dreams
We see its shadowy shape and hear the surge
    Roll sobbing on its sands, but no sails skim
    The sea which round its silver scarping gleams.

THE THREE QUEENS.

Clad in their lily robes came fair queens three
    And stood upon the verge, with palms to eyes,
    Searching the bluest rim of those blue skies
For some ships sailing o'er the azure sea
From the dim outer world: then sharp drew she,
    The stateliest one, breath quickened with thin sighs:
    She saw but sea-gulls from the pale foam rise
And shadows broadening on the sandy lea.
And one was tall and crowned upon the head,
    And one was like a lily blowing fair,
    The other seemed most like lost loves and sweet,
To men's sad sight, re-risen from the dead.
    So stood they with the nimbus round their hair,
    And sea-foam shining wet against their feet.

THE SHEPHERDS.

Leave, Daphnis, leave thy snowy flocks to feed
    On long slopes lush with dew, or by the rill
    Sweet honey-bells to crop, roving at will
Thro' shadowy brake and rose-emblossomed mead
And where pale lilies star the water-weed.
    See, how moonbeams the dusky valleys fill
    With pallid fire: Bring, then, thy polished quill,
Thy flocks thy shepherd's crook no longer need.
Here on a bank with daffodils o'erspread,
    Our weary limbs at ease we will recline
And try who from the reed's smooth-jointed bore
The sweeter strains can draw. This conch-shell red
    The prize shall be. Now let the strain divine
    Float echoing o'er the dim Thessalian shore.

CASTLES IN SPAIN.

Castles in Spain! they nothing cost, and I
    Therefore all mine will build stately and fair,
    Bedight with pearl and gold and ivory rare,
With diamond towers reared 'gainst a blue-bowed sky;
It shall in silks, marbles, and carved-work vie
    With Cleopatra's fabled palace; there
    Shall loiter lilied streams; beyond compare
Its palmy courts and esplanades shall lie;
And there for pleasure and for beauty fain,
    Gay dames and gentlemen shall come and go;
    In song and dance and amorous dalliance, fleet
    The moon-led hours shall unremembered flow
To soft accompaniment of citernes sweet:
    But sad guests shall not near my bright demain.

P. M. H.

Is it not thou,—thine eyes, thy face? But, nay—
    Too strangely wan! I scarcely know if dream
    Of fancy shaped thee to my sight: I seem
As one who, waking at the day-spring gray,
A shape that wandered down the star-sown way
    Recalls in musing sweet. O must I deem
    Thee lost to life, or risen in the gleam
Of that clear dawn which marks immortal day?
In the vast shade and silence of the night,
    Is it thou, thy very self? With that same smile
    Thou wast wont to brave the fierceness of thy pain!
O shadow, shadow, to my wistful sight
    Be real man, if only for the while
    That serves to calm the o'er-wrought heart and brain!

POLYPHEME TO THE NYMPH GALATEA.

AFTER THEOCRITUS.

Come, Galatea, from thy sea-blue caves,
Forsake the sobbing billow, leave the waves
That wash forever round their shell-built walls
And beat with restless surge thy coral halls,
For these, sweet nymph, in nothing can compare
With the demains that thou with me shalt share.
The fields invite thee, where the crocus spreads
Its golden mesh, where glowing poppy beds
Await the pastimes of our joyful loves;
And, in green coverts, flocks of crooning doves
From morn to noon-tide mourn withheld delight,
From noon to twilight mourn, but all the night
Sad Philomel unto the yellow moon
Utters her lovelorn plaint; for her too soon
The dayspring flushes red the dewy East.
Come, Galatea, where the brown bees feast
On the thin nectar of the Asphodel,
Or, dipping deep into some wild-rose bell,
Make themselves drunk with sweets: O sea-maid, here
Thou mayst trip nimbly, without sense of fear;
The wanton Triton shall not thee pursue
When gleams the moonlight on the darkling blue,
Nor dread Poseidon from his kingly chayre
Leaning too lowly, with caresses scare;
No hippodame, vaulting the wave's white crest,
Make thy heart beat affrighted in thy breast;
But, alike protected from the Sea-king's lure,
And from warlike or bestial force secure,

Thou shalt abide with me among the groves,
Where chaste Diana in the shadow roves,
With slender bow and swift suspended dart
Seeking unweariedly the antlered hart,
Her buskined nymphs attending at her side.
The hounds' deep clamor thro' the woods rings wide,
What time the silver crescent o'er the hills
Low hanging, with white fire the valley fills.
The rosy Oreads shall thy companions be,
And Dryads, bursting from the rough-rinded tree;
But the laughing Satyr and the dancing Faun
And wild Bacchants that greet the silver dawn
With rites licentious, crowned with ivy vine
And pouring out libations of red wine,
These, Galatea, shall not thee molest,
Nor break with wanton sport thy dewy rest.
Here in the rocky cave shalt thou repose
On beds of dusky hyacinth and rose;
Here will I bring thee fruits to eat, and curds,
With milk newly taken from my mottled herds:
In summer thou shalt wear lawn garments thin,
And scarlet wool in winter thou shalt spin:
And when the flocks return at close of day
Sweetly for thee my tuneful pipes I'll play.
Come, Galatea, from thy sea-blue caves,
Forsake the unstable ocean's foamy wave.

SIR OWEN AND LADY ELINED.

A song of the Lady Elined;
She looked across the white and red,
Her falcon fretted at the jess;—
She sighed for very idleness.

Far down, and thro' the golden wheat
There came the croon of wood-doves sweet;
Far down, upon the reedy shore,
She counted six white swans, and more:

The white swans spread their rustling snow
And sailed away, six in a row;
The falcon fretted at the jess;—
She sighed for very idleness.

" I've coiffed my long locks' wandering gold,
I've made straight every silvery fold
Of my thin gown of pale samite;
With seed-pearls is my girdle dight:

But when there are no eyes aware,
What matter tho' a maid be fair?''
The falcon fretted at the jess;—
She sighed for very weariness.

Across the beds of daffodils
She saw the violet of the hills;
Beyond the tawny fields of corn
She heard a huntsman wind his horn.

He rode across the low green plain;
Cool shone the grasses after rain;
He saw the river's silver edge
Gleam thro' the fringe of emerald sedge;

He saw above the banks aflower
A castle's battlemented tower;
Upon the battlement, so fair
He saw the gleam of golden hair.

She heard a huntsman wind his horn,
She saw him spur across the corn;
Her falcon fretted at the jess—
She sighed no more for weariness.

"Come down, O true love mine, come down:
Strong lances wait in yonder town;
My scarlet pennon floats the breeze,
I have fair ships on many seas."

"Well guarded are the doors, Sir Knight,
The brazen bolts are drawn up tight,
A hundred lances guard the hall,
The bloodhounds lie without the wall."

"Loose, me, my true love, loose thy veil—
My arms are strong—they will not fail;
My barb is swift, o'er dale and down
We'll ride to yonder small fair town."

"I have no veil, Sir Owen fair,
I'll loose to thee my coiffed hair."
Her falcon breaking from the jess
Soared free into the wilderness.

She's slit her gown of pale samite,
She's twisted ropes so silken slight:
"Now in the corn go bide, my lord,
Till I have twisted strong the cord."

The sun sank low, the sun sank red,
Fair Elined rose from her bed;
She took the rope so silken slight
And slid adown the castle height.

Across the fields of yellow wheat
They rode away on palfrey fleet;
By glade and glen, both fast and far,
Beneath the mellow morning star.

And coming hard by the high sea-down
Beheld the spires of a small fair town;
And there they saw the ships asail
Before the pleasant morning gale:

And there they saw the pennons fly
Scarlet against the pearl-white sky:
Fourscore fair youths in velvet coats
Abode in harbour with the boats.

They sailed across the foaming seas,
With scarlet floating on the breeze,
And nevermore twixt white and red,
Saw they the Lady Elined.

Far in his castled northern isle
He's brought his lady wife the while;
With fête and tournament and play,
His knights made glad the wedding day.

Two-score damsels of high degree,
Weaving borders of broiderie
On gowns of satin and sendal,
Attended the lady in the hall.

Full many a minstrel, harping south,
Sang to her praise with sweetest mouth;
Full many a minstrel east and west,
Sang of Sir Owen and his quest.

TO LALAGE.

Clear as a star,
    In her blue heaven burning,
Serene, unattainable, afar,
(Oh, in my heaven a star,)
Thou dwellest where seraphs are,
    While I behold thee, yearning,
Clear as a star,
    In her blue heaven burning.

THE SINGER OF SONGS.

Tho' I should go all night
Thro' the gardens, plucking the roses,
I should ne'er have flowers enough,
E'en tho' I should go all night
Thro' the gardens, plucking the roses.

The roses dream on the bush,
And the Queen-moon dreams above,
The breezes dream in the apple boughs,
There's none awake but I.

No one awake but I,
Who forever make new songs;
And tho' I should sing the whole night thro',
I should never have songs enough,
Who forever make new songs.

The moonlight silvers the rose,
And the silent fountain gleams
Like the Cyclop's single eye:
Shall I sing of the red, red rose,
Or the white rose, chill with dew,
Or shall I sing of the moonlight there,
The fig leaves shining thro'?

But tho' I should spend the night
In plucking the red, red roses,
I should ne'er have roses enough;
And tho' I should sing the whole night thro',
To my lute with the silver strings,
I should never have songs enough
For my lute with the silver strings.

THE GRAVESTONE.

The rain is on the myrtle bush,
The wind sighs in the dusky leaves,
And, splash, upon the white gravestone,
The great drops fall, like tears;
The rain beats down the hyacinths,
And cuts the young grass spears in twain —
I wonder if he hears it fall,
Down in the narrow coffin there,
Or if the cold drops siping thro',
Trouble his last dreams?

Between two clouds just now, the moon
Looked out; long rays of silver slid
Down the wet shimmering mist, and gleamed
Across that white gravestone;
I saw the carved name—"Paul," it read—
'Tis one year since he died.

And since he died, it seems so strange
Any should be alive:
I see the men he used to know
Walk smiling in the thronging streets,
And I myself look at the sun,
Rejoicing in its pleasant light;
But when the rain is on the bush,
And thro' the mist the gravestone gleams,
When I am weary of my cares,
And sick at heart and out of tune,
Oh, then I think of him out there,
With gladness that for him 'tis done,

And wish the time were come for me
To lie beneath a white headstone;
Perhaps the rain then on the bush
Would make the dreaming seem more sweet:
I know not that, but this is true,
Life's full of storm and gloom and rain,
And all beyond is mystery;
I know not whether souls live on
In other spheres of joy or pain,
Or whether death be but a sleep
Beneath the rain-wet hyacinths
And sobbing myrtle leaves.

ACROSS THE AWN.

Across the awn I saw Love flee,
　　And dip the silver dawn,
Between the wan moon and the sea,
　　Across the awn.

Behold, here are but shadows drawn,
　　Of bleaching bud and tree,
Across the hoar rime of the lawn;

These only has he left to me,
　　With wildered ghosts and thrawn,
Sad things and shadowy shapes to see,
　　Across the awn.

THE LADY OF THE CASTLE.

She sitteth in the castle tower
　　(Woe is me and wel-a-way),
Twining a wreath of the lily flower;
　　Ever she doth weep and say,
　　"Woe is me and wel-a-way,"
Twining a wreath of the lily flower.

She hath bound a lily to her hair
　　(Woe is me and wel-a-way),
She than lilies far more fair;
　　Ever she doth sigh and say
　　"Woe is me and wel-a-way,"
She than lilies far more fair.

She lists the moon-face far on high
　　(Woe is me and wel-a-way),
"Sweet lady of the violet sky,
　　Hast thou a lover fain to stray,
　　Woe is me and wel-a-way,
Sweet lady of the violet sky?"

An ivory lute with silver strings
　　(Woe is me and wel-a-way)
She hath, to which she sadly sings,
　　In the gloaming of the day,
　　"Woe is me and wel-a-way,"
Unto her lute she sadly sings.

CYMIDIS.

Be pleased, Immortals, now my steps to guide
Where Cymidis and gentle oreads hide,
For I have sought the wanderer in vain;
And now the sun, returning after rain,
Has dried the twinkling mosses by the streams,
And soon the stars will bring the hour of dreams:
Whom should I seek when balmy dews descend
And purple flames with flames of silver blend?

Thee, Cymidis; beneath the burning blue,
Mid columbines and violets late and few,
Oft sought and seldom found, where laughing strife
Of fleeing nymphs and sylvan gods was rife,
And cross the drowsy air the tender flute
Of Doric shepherds did mine ears salute.

What tho' Apollo urged his golden car,
His arrows pierced not thro' the snowy bar,
And flaming oaks spread wide their scarlet tent,
With yellow poplars, all their broideries rent;
There Shrinx sighed, wildered, in the tawny shade,
And, "love, O love," the wood-doves pined and prayed.

And all that thou, too wary, mightst return
To thy soft couch, o'er which slim willows burn
Torch-like against the turquoise firmament;
Where amorous dreams from ivory sun-gates sent,
Lull to forgetfulness the wistful soul,
Consenting to the Cyprian's sweet control.

Thus, Cymidis, by fruitless quest I find,
Thou wilt not with thy silken fillet bind
The frivolous or wine-mad reveller;
Thou lov'st the covert thick of bay and fir:
O when wan Cynthia, wearied on the hills
Rests her huge tire, and by the mellow rills
One plaintive bird divulges all her woe,
Then comest thou, Cymidis, with foot-step slow,
And there requitals make to all that grieve
At loss of love, the Parcae's late reprieve.

APRIL SONG.

Vert leaves sigh in the breezes again,
    Oh Sweetheart,
Frogs croak softly in meadow and fen,
    Oh Sweetheart,
And gay-vested tulips as I pass
Fling up their fragrance from the grass,
    Sweetheart, my sweet.

And there is the moon at the end of the way,
    Oh Sweetheart,
Holding her red torch up: but nay,
    Oh Sweetheart,
There is no need of Love's torch-light
To show us the desolate paths to-night,
    Sweetheart, my sweet.

THE WRAITH VOYAGEUR.

I rode on the hills in my chariot of fire,
    As I rode the slopes were aglow;
The mad winds muttered a wicked desire,
    The thrawn woods whispered low.

With wheels of white silver I rode on the sea,
    As I rode the billows were pale;
The surges sang in unholy glee,
    The sea-gull uplifted its sail:

And far on the waves beneath me afloat
    Were tresses of golden hair;
On the long reef lay a black-hulled boat,
    The sea-gulls hovered there.

The wreck of a schooner, a golden tress,
    On the waves a quavering wail;
Was that the cry of the sea-gull? Confess,
    The sea-gull winged with a sail?

I rode upon seas of amethyst bright,
    As the morning star sank low;
The wind was a bugle hailing the light,
    The crisp foam gleamed like snow.

I saw far afloat o'er the crystal deep
    A dead girl, naked and fair;
She lay on the waves like a sea-nymph asleep
    In the sheen of her golden hair.

THE WEARY HOURS.

Oh, wearily, wearily now the rain
Beats on the roof, beats on the pane,
Wearily, wearily.

Wearily from their unseen towers
Bells make count of the leaden hours,
Wearily, wearily.

SONG OF FAREWELL.

The blue-bird and the robin both have flown,
Sweetheart,
And fiercely on the northern storm-winds blown,
The leaves all swart,
Are scattered o'er the river's tuneless brink;
Pale dandelions down the chill gales sink,
The skies are dim, the sunbeams wan and sheer;
I sit among the wasted leaves and think
Of thee, my dear.

So anxious with the birds to be away,
Sweetheart,
And like them fain the wanderer to play;
Glad to depart
With other light o' loves, on idle quests;
Alas, like birds that leave their empty nests,
Thy thoughts already fly drear leagues from me,
And leave me midst the old year's mournful guests.
To weep for thee.

SONGS, SONNETS AND BALLADS.

CHILEELI.

Oh hear, 'tis the Chileeli,
The golden-throated,
Musician of a single strain;
In the dim twilight of the cedar tree
He sings of love,
And death.

Oh hear, 'tis the Chileeli,
The messenger of love:
He sings 'neath sun and moon.
In the dim twilight of the whispering pines.
The pale seas murmur to the pines,
The dim pines whisper sadly to the seas,
But the Chileeli, under sun and moon.
Sings to the heart
Of love.

Chileeli, sweet,
Behold the sun is gone,
Chileeli, love,
The flag-flowers by the sea
Wave purple over Menimonee's grave;
Sing then no more of long-lost loves,
Ah, sing no more of pain;
See, how the moon floats on the shining wave,
And the sea-gull guides my slender birch canoe:
Sing then of joy,
Of new delights.
Chileeli, Oh Chileeli,
Thou wondrous bird.

ARABESQUES.

Outside, the summer noon upon the wheat lies hot.
White sunbeams shimmer on the rosy garden plot,
The ringdoves croon in cool, close coverts by the stream;
But here the green light lies subdued as in a dream.
Around the latticed window wreathed with flowering
     vines,
The honey bees drowse lazily; with checkered lines
Leaf shadows faintly etch the floor; soft zephyrs strew
Perfumes; beyond the window gleams a strip of blue.
Outside, the summer noontide, splendid, hot, and white;
Within, the dreamy silence and the cloistered light;
The couch diaphanous, with silken covers spread,
Invites repose, an eider cushion neath the head:
Sleep's fillet, loosely drawn about my weary brow,
Now lets fantastic dreams, and antic fancies now,
Creep neath my half-closed eye-lids, and still half
     awake
I see the arras in the wandering south winds shake:
The silken arras, woven of many a thread of green,
Shot thro' with crimson bars, and golden strands
     between;
Thereon strange figures float, waver, and bend, and
     sway,
Dance madly forth, retire, and rise and fall away:
Rich oriental blossoms star the broidered hem,
Citron, lotus, and rose, and, on its broken stem,
The passion-flower: and there the moody stork pursues
His solemn thoughts, mid shallows of Milesian blues.

Far from his native haunts along the reedy shore,
He stands disconsolate, lamenting that no more
With twisted neck, on the sea-marsh's dreary edge,
He seeks the torpid crab and oyster in the sedge,
And, clinging to the briny weed, shell-fish and snail:
Beyond the frothing surf one single snowy sail
Flies like a shining sea-bird o'er the violet deep,
But as the sun descends, his embers steep
Its fluttering plumes in flame; so from the charmed
    sight
It sinks at last below the shadowy verge of night:
Back from their secret caves the darkening waters pour,
And round the jagged rocks the foaming surges roar;
But Silence hovers o'er the salt and sallow marsh;
Here comes not oar, or sail, or shout of sailor harsh;
The night wind in the weeds and slim reeds whistles
    low,
The bittern cries across the moaning tide's outflow,
And, sheltered in the cypress tree's funereal arms,
The owl, with hollow cries, the lonely night alarms,
And thro' her fleecy vail, the broad-faced, wistful moon
Sees in the wimpling pools her wrinkled image swoon.
Still does the solemn stork, sedate, attenuate,
Upon his one leg stand, moody, disconsolate,
Musing, perchance, on bygone days, replete with bliss,
More than a hundred hoary years removed from this.

THE LADY OF CONWAY LEA.

The bridegroom's hall was garnished fair
    With rose and eglantine,
And merry was the feast that night,
    And goodly was the wine:

The bride was decked in diamond stones,
    And clad in silk array:
She lightly rose from the bridegroom's side,
    Before the dawn of day.

Before the watchet dawn of day,
    By dripping field and dell;
"Oh, tell me, whither goest thou?"
    "To yonder small chapelle;

"For I a wedding hymn would sing,
    And I a prayer would say,
In yon chapelle upon the hill,
    Before the break of day."

Then came the bridegroom forth in haste,
    And summoned his household;
The groomsmen and the bridemaids came,
    And men two-hundred told.

"What man is true and bold," saith he,
    "For by St. Christopher,
This jewel fair I'll give to him
    That findeth trace of her."

Hard ran the guests and servitors,
    And scoured the country round;
A score of miles they rode and ran;
    No lady could be found.

*   *   *   *   *   *   *   *   *

Who is this pale and sweet ladye?
    She lieth on her bed,
Her body lieth wan and weak,
    And droopeth her sad head:

Her dark eyes glow beneath her brows,
    She speaketh ever low;
"Oh, when my bodye's dead, I charge
    To Conway thou wilt go.

For there my husband waiteth me;
    Twelve weary years hath he
Dwelt lonely in the castle hall,
    Where first he wedded me.

In loving life have I been thine,
    (A love tho' not a wife),
But now the grave that's waiting me
    Shall be the end of strife."

He took her hand and kissed so sweet,
    He groaned aloud with pain;
"This sore disease hath taken her,
    And grief hath crazed her brain.

Oh, we were wedded in yon chapelle,
    Between marshland and lea,
And man and wife we rode that day
    To Sandys by the sea."

Upon her cheeks of blanchéd snow
    Came out the color red;
"Wedded with one I was, but thou
    Wert not the man," she said.

"Now by the love thou bearest me,
    And by the soul I gave,
I charge thee, bring the holy man
    To shrive me for the grave.

And if my ghost would kindly rest
    When of my bodye free,
My grave must be made wide and deep,
    At Towers of Conway Lea."

His hands cling close to her pale hands,
    With grief falleth his head;
"Nay, how may I withstand thy will?
    Thy sweet ghost rest," he said.

Now bring the coffin and the pall,
    Put off the diamond bands,
And clothe her in a shroud of lawn,
    And clasp her slender hands,

In mute prayer, as she lieth still
    Among her maidens weeping;
Now Jesu pardon her soul's sin,
    And give her peaceful sleeping.

*   *   *   *   *   *   *   *   *   *

Oh, sweetly now the summer moon,
    The full red moon of June,
Shone o'er the ships that spread their sails,
    At sound o' the sailors' tune:

Oh, broadly now the summer moon,
　　Of soft and ruddy blee,
Shone o'er the dusky roofs and towers
　　Of Sandys by the sea:

And softly from the rose-gardens
　　That line the milk-white way,
Oh, sweetly from the gardens rang
　　The nightingale's sad lay:

Oh, sadly down the dim, white way,
　　With sobs instead of song
The dead-train o' the wan ladye
　　Wound solemnly along.

And woe it was for Lord St. John,
　　He rode at head o' the train,
With black upon his haughty crest,
　　And drooping plumes amain.

At Conway gates he stopped and rung;
　　Quoth the ancient senechal,
"What cavalcade before the gate,
　　At dark midnight doth call?

A great lord, by his haughty crest,
　　And a dead-train at his back;
At my time o' life, what is it to me
　　To get me down, alack,

And open the door to a phantom train?"
　　Quoth the ancient senechal:
Then down he got to the castle gate
　　And answered the horseman's call.

Uprose in haste from his pillow
    The Lord of Conway Lea,
And forthwith out of his bedchamber,
    (With dead flowers decked) went he.

"Who is it calleth at my gate?"
    "I am the Lord St. John."
"Why comest thou to my castle gate?"
    "My oath I act upon:

For so I vowed to my ladye dead,
    At Towers of Conway Lea,
When Death her soul had from it taken,
    Her bodye should buried be."

Down from his dark-housed steed he got;
    His followers void of fear,
With shoulders bent for burthening,
    Lowered the ladye's bier,

"Oh, whose this face that I look on,
    This face so dear to me?"
And sadly fell his hot tears o'er
    The face o' the wan ladye.

He hath kissed her on the cheeks and lips,
    He hath called her name aloud;
"Oh, why hast thou returned to me
    In coffin and in shroud?"

Then up and spake the Lord St. John
    To him of Conway Lea,
"With this broadsword that's at my thigh,
    I'll strike through thy bodye."

"I pray thee tell what meaneth this,
  For by St. Christopher,
This is my wife, twelve years agone
  'Fore all I married her."

"A lie," fierce answered Lord St. John,
  "By book and e'en by bell,
Wedded were we at dawn o' day,
  In yonder small chapelle."

Oh, there was fierce fighting that night,
  At Towers of Conway Lea,
Oh, there was stain of bloody gore
  Where no blood-stain should be.

And one fell riven through the head,
  T'other thro' the breast;
Around them fell their men-at-arms,
  Bleeding and sore distressed.

But at the dawning o' the day
  Uprose the Lord St. John,
And dragged him to the purple bier
  His ladye lay upon.

His cheek pressed cold against her cheek,
  His limbs sank cold and prone,
Oh, gayly on his dying brow
  The red sunlight shone.

The men-at-arms, some got them up
  And staunched their flowing wounds,
And some lay stark, oh, ne'er again
  To waken from their swounds.

Then groaned the ancient senechal,
  "Ah, woe this day to see,
My lord is slain, the staff is broke
  This day in Conway Lea."

He brought the wine and bandages,
  He took up his master,
And bore him into the castle hall
  Upon his bent shoulder.

Long wept the Lord of Conway Lea,
  "Would God I too were slain,
And lying buried in the grave
  Wherein her bodye's lain.

Oh never in the fair, green land,
  Was one more fair than she,
Her silken locks were braided broad,
  And tawny was her e'e.

Oh never in the good, green land,
  Bloomed any flower so fair,
Like twin-blown lilies were her cheeks,
  And tawny was her hair."

THE ANGEL OF DELIVERANCE.

And he that stood upon the bar of gold,
    I saw his form against the blue like fire;
Beneath him clouds of vivid purple rolled,
      And voices of the sweet eternal choir
      Breathed tender anthems; o'er the blue, like fire
The heavenly hosts ranged, rank on rank untold.

Tall as the northern pine, in shining white,
    About his garment's hem embroidered bells
In golden silk were wrought, with tracery slight
      Of leaves and vines and flowering asphodels,
      With golden fringes and embroidered bells,
And round his breast an emerald girdle plight.

His face was like a star that nightly steeps
    The midmost space in glory, and his eyes,
That pierced eternal mysteries, their deeps
      Had drunk immortal splendors, the wrapt skies
      Were hushed beneath the marvel of his eyes;
His look was that of one who joys and weeps.

His holy brow, within his shadowy hair
    Was smooth as ivory, and meekness, blent
With solemn majesty, was throned there;
      And his stern lips apart were softly bent,
      Thereon and love and tenderness were blent,
As when one smiles between two words of prayer.

Within his outstretched hand a flaming brand,
    Keen as the lightning that divides the cloud,
He held uplifted o'er the shadowy land;

On distant peaks behind him, crowd on crowd
Of shining seraphs shore aside the cloud;
Their purple wings the mellow twilight fanned.

And downward won a chorus thin and sweet
    From those clear heights behind the blazing sun,
As should the Angelus the dawning greet,
    So from on high the tender chorus won,
    Thrilling the air behind the blazing sun,
And making distant heights the strain repeat.

Faint harps and dulcimers of golden strings
    Made interlude melodious and soft,
And as those hosts waved wide their iris wings,
    Thro' sunny depths of space sweeping aloft,
    The air was drenched with wandering perfume, soft
As that which round Gul's crimson garden clings.

Then he that stood upon the burning bar
    Put to his lips a gleaming ivory horn;
The sonorous notes dispersed themselves afar;
    Straightway it seemed as if all sad things born
    Entrancéd heard his sonorous ivory horn,
And joyed to hear all sorrowing things that are.

For prison doors wide from their grim bolts flew,
    And yawning graves gave up their ghostly dead,
The scroll of heaven came as morning blue,
    And every wail on earth was silencéd:
    For every empty arm received its dead,
And all the world laughed as when life was new.

And every barren place with harvests smiled,
    And purple fruits o'erhung the silver streams;
The rugged paths with roses were beguiled,
    The glory was the glory of sweet dreams;
    Blue lotus flowers grew lush along the streams,
And laburnum flamed o'er the hoary wild.

All they that had been old grew young once more,
    And faces that had furrowed been with tears
Renewed their bloom, and pallid foreheads wore
    The solemn nimbus of immortal years;
    Old sorrows vanished and old rains of tears,
And old regrets their tyranny forswore.

From sunlight unto moonlight songbirds sang,
    From moonlight unto sunlight sweethearts pined
In love's sweet ecstacy; the high vault rang
    All night with happy song: on beds reclined
    Of rose and poppy, pensive sweethearts pined,
Singing to lute and dulcimer of love's dear pang.

The vision changed; along the violet verge
    Descended shapes which seemed like seraphim;
On wings of flame cleaving the starry surge,
    They crossed the skies and on the utmost rim
    Sank from the sight, and other seraphim
I saw likewise between the stars emerge.

Then fell clear voices down the pulseless calm
    Of violet space; such voices as we hear
Between the Easter lily and the palm;

Afar, then coming nearer and more near,
Sounded such fluting voices as we hear
On Easter morn, chanting a holy psalm.

And at the sound a perfect sweet content
Was transfused thro' this weary sorrowing heart;
Weary, sorrowing, with want and woe forspent,
And frenzied still with Grief's despairing smart,
Now through this sick, tormented, sorrowing heart,
The joy of heavenly satisfaction went.

I saw again the ivory evening star
Shed thro' the saffron west its lambent light,
And o'er the trailing aureoles afar
The strong, tall angel, clad in shining white;
I scarce might know his plumage from starlight,
Or from past sunsets his bright scimetar.

Joy shook my pulses and my awed soul thrilled
With shock of heavenly passion; as I kneeled
I heard above the splash of founts that spilled
Their spray upon the dusk, soft bells which pealed
Adown the violet silence, as I kneeled,
The shadowy vale with melody was filled.

*   *   *   *   *   *   *   *   *   *

The pilgrim kneeled, with face pressed to the dew,
His tranced sight filled with splendor of high dreams;
Perchance the angel soared beyond the blue,
Or mayhap, as some clearer vision deems,
Remained with him, the substance of his dreams,
The forerunner of Heaven's retinue.

DIANA.

Her face peers weirdly o'er the gabled roof,
　　She scatters flakes of silver on the eaves,
Then draws about her brows the cloud's dark woof,
　　And listens to the wind-harp in the leaves.

Anon she flings the cloudy veil aside,
　　And shines forth in her beauty clear and keen;
Thro' azure gulfs of glory sailing wide,
　　She fills all earth and heaven with her sheen.

DANDELIONS.

In May, the dandelions with rich gold
　　Spangled the sunny satin-smooth green swards;
In July-prime, grown wistful, wan and old,
　　They are the lazy south-wind's tender wards.

The lazy south-wind tempts the airy whorls,
　　With soft caresses, murmurs and beguiles,
Till each, o'ercome, its spirit plume unfurls
　　And floats away to unknown faery isles.

Lo, on the blue they spread their silken wings,
　　And sail away to faery lands unseen;
While still the south-wind in the poplar sings,
　　And still the sun mellows the plundered green.

THE SHEPHERD BOY.

The shepherd boy has left his fleecy flocks,
To follow Daphne of the shining locks:
   Return, return, O shepherd, to thy fold,
   And run not after wandering fires of gold.

The shepherd boy has found the fair-faced maid,
And woos her neath the fragrant myrtle shade:
   And now his snowy flocks uncared-for feed
   In tangled woods, or on the oft-cropped mead.

BURNING BOUGHS.

Gay scarlet burns among the leaves,
   The oak uplifts its flaming brand;
But silhouetted on the sky,
   The shadowy Pollard willows stand.

The wind drives hard the whirling snow
   Of clouds across the violet,
And in each pine and burning bough,
   A sweetly thrilling harp is set.

NARCISSUS.

It fell that on a shining summer's day
When wearied with the hunt, beside the way
Narcissus found a tranquil silver lake,
And leaning down, his eager thirst to slake,
(With limbs outstretched upon the silky grass),
Beheld his image in the liquid glass.
His tender cheek still wore the floret's bloom,
As red as roses' carmine; the tawny gloom
Of the stag's eyes when in terror rolled,
Beneath his full-fringed eyelids showed; red gold
Gleamed in his wind-tossed curls; his dewy mouth
Was like a pouting rose, when as the south
Has warmed its beauty ripe; more white than milk
His tender skin, more smooth than woven silk;
His polished limbs, stretched carelessly along
The herbage green, were delicate and strong;
No godlike charm or beauty did he lack,
His charms the waters smooth reflected back.
His own sweet image then he deemed the form
Of some shy naiad, with young beauty warm,
And he who had fond Echo's love denied,
Nor heeded when upon the hills she cried
His name beloved, now felt most fierce desire
Burn in his veins like a consuming fire.
Narcissus, lovely, rash and foolish boy,
Thee would the fierce Olympians destroy!
See, how he languishes, and now he bends
Above the inconstant flood, and now he rends

His golden locks, and tenderly complains
Of her, who, longing, yet his love disdains.
To her he promise makes of every toy,
And to his heaving breast strives clasp the coy
Illusive form deemed virginal and fit
His warm embraces to sustain; and lit
With glowing fires, his troubled soft young eyes
He lifts to heaven, and lamentably sighs.
At last, with love and vain desires o'ercome,
He sinks upon the ground, with anguish dumb,
And rests his pale cheek on his arms, and weeps;
His gilded locks in salty dew he steeps,
Scarce old enough of tears to be ashamed:
While she, of all young nymphs the gentlest named,
Fond Echo, grieving in his grief, would bring
New milk and honey fresh, striving the sting
From sorrow's wound to pluck; but in a pet,
With bitter words he drives her off, tho' yet
She patient lingers near, and from the hill
Shares in his melancholy vigil still.

 * * * * * * * * * *

Now Phoebus down the blue steep swiftly rides,
And thro' the eastern gates pale Silene glides;
Now Hera o'er the flowery fields and dales
The bright dew flings, and Zephyrus soft gales
Sets free o'er groves and slopes, and many a train
Of glittering stars treads down the skyey plain;
But still the youth upon the grasses lies,
And still fond Echo answers his low cries:
Anon, o'ercome of love and grief, he stoops
Amid pale lilies and the tangled loops

Of purple flag, and, where the ripple breaks
Beneath the moon in scattered silver flakes,
Again beholds his image in the stream.
These tender eyes, as in a hallowed dream,
Give answer back, with longing smile for smile,
And unto bliss ineffable beguile;
And, wistful neath the tangled golden curls,
This face looks at him from the shining purls:
The youth embraces coral lip to lip,
And feels the soft shape from his fond arms slip;
Now panting, eager, he in vain would hold
The loved illusion which his arms enfold;
Beneath his arms the yielding water flies,
And from his sight the tender image dies.
Like a frail flower o'erblown in wildest gales,
When thunders sound along the hollow vales,
And Zeus far his flaming fire-bolt hurls
Across the mountain where the thick rain whirls,
The boy once more sinks on the rushes prone,
Upon his famished lips a stifled moan
A moment stirs the forest's silent rest.
With face into the dewy grasses pressed,
At last he lies, quite motionless and still,
While timid Echo watches from the hill,
And Silene, stooping from her wandering chair,
Lays silvery touches on his silky hair.

     *   *   *   *   *   *   *   *   *   *

Unto this spot came woodnymphs on a day,
Their limbs to lave and in the shade to play.
"Who lieth here?" cried one, and whispering made
Her fellows hide within the deeper shade;

Their conference with speech and gesture swift
They held, beholding thro' a narrow rift
Within the boughs the boy hid in the sedge
Which lushly grew upon the fountain's edge:
At length emboldened by his silence they
The thicket left and crossed the grassy way.
The fleetest nymph and tallest of the band
Came first, and bending, laid her snowy hand
Upon the dreamer's head, and smoothing light
The many-clustered curls, pressed kisses slight
Upon the lad's pale cheek: an icy chill
Smote thro' her rosy lips and sent a thrill
Of fear into her heart; for aid she cried,
And all her fellows came and with her tried
To wake the slumbering youth; and in their arms
Uplifted him, and sought with all great charms
His senses to restore; and one caressed
And held him closely to her bosom pressed,
Another chafed his hands, another drew
The stiffened eyelids from his meek eyes blue;
And one took water in her doubled palm
And sprinkled his wan brow, and some with balm
Of healing herbs anointed him. . . . . In vain.
About him knelt the beauteous bright-eyed train,
With locks dishevelled, and with many tears
Bewailing his fair looks and tender years:
"Alas, sweet Narcisse, O alas the boy,
What cruel god did thus his darts employ
To lay thee low? and ah, alas the hour
That stole from thee thy young life's happy dower."
And thus in many honied words of grief
They sought to give their gentle hearts relief,

While constant Echo from her caverns still
Made ring the forests and the bosky hill.
Then she the tallest and the fairest one
Arose and turned toward the failing sun;
His last beams stained her marble shoulders pink
And warmed the fountain's chill and misty brink,
And touched with flame the dead boy lying there,
With halos brightening his brow and hair:
"Ye heavenly powers" (the tender woodnymph prayed)
"Who dwell on high Olympas, undismayed,
Who on Olympas dwell, from every woe
Forevermore exempt, who cannot know
The grief of mortals, ever made to bend
Beneath the yoke of sorrows without end:
O Mercury, thou shepherd strong of souls,
Who leadeth safely thro' the darkening shoals
Of that sad river underneath the earth:
And thou who watcheth, goddess, at the birth
Of tender babes, Ye powers that rule above
And no less rule below, all ye that love
The gentle race of men, we thee implore
Give young Narcissus to our arms once more!
See, where he lies, the beauteous one, all cold
And pale and helpless, who was once so bold
In war and chase, who made the forests ring
With joyous shouts; who knew also to sing
And sweetly play the seven-jointed reed!
Alas, our voice no longer does he heed,
But lies all mute and helpless on the edge
Of this lone fountain, mid the whispering sedge.
Well was he loved by men and rosy maids,
And by the nymphs who haunt the oaken shades,

Ye loved him also; heavenly powers restore
The young Narcissus to our arms once more."
She ceased, and as the shades began to fall
Her fellows with her spread a leafy pall
Upon the dead youth's form, and so withdrew
To watch until the morrow's morning blue
Should break in glory o'er the eastern sky.

*   *   *   *   *   *   *   *   *   *

And now when Phoebus' car ascended high
The nymphs again unto the fountain went,
And in a roseate glowing circle bent
Above the leafy pall which they had spread.
Lo, there no longer lay the lovely dead,
But where his head had lain, a starry bloom
Gleamed mid the green of leaves, and all the gloom
Of sighing woods was filled with perfume. Thus
Sprang first the shining flower, the Narcissus.